故園畫憶

庚寅中秋 韓磬泉 題

《故园画忆系列》编委会

名誉主任：韩启德

主　　任：邵　鸿

委　　员：（按姓氏笔画为序）

万　捷	王秋桂	方李莉	叶培贵
刘魁立	况　晗	严绍璗	吴为山
范贻光	范　芳	孟　白	邵　鸿
岳庆平	郑培凯	唐晓峰	曹兵武

故园画忆系列
MEMORY OF THE OLD
Home in Sketches

天山南部风情
Style in South of Tianshan Mountains

孟福利　徐敬龙　绘画
孟福利　撰文
Sketches by Meng Fuli & Xu Jinglong
Notes by Meng Fuli

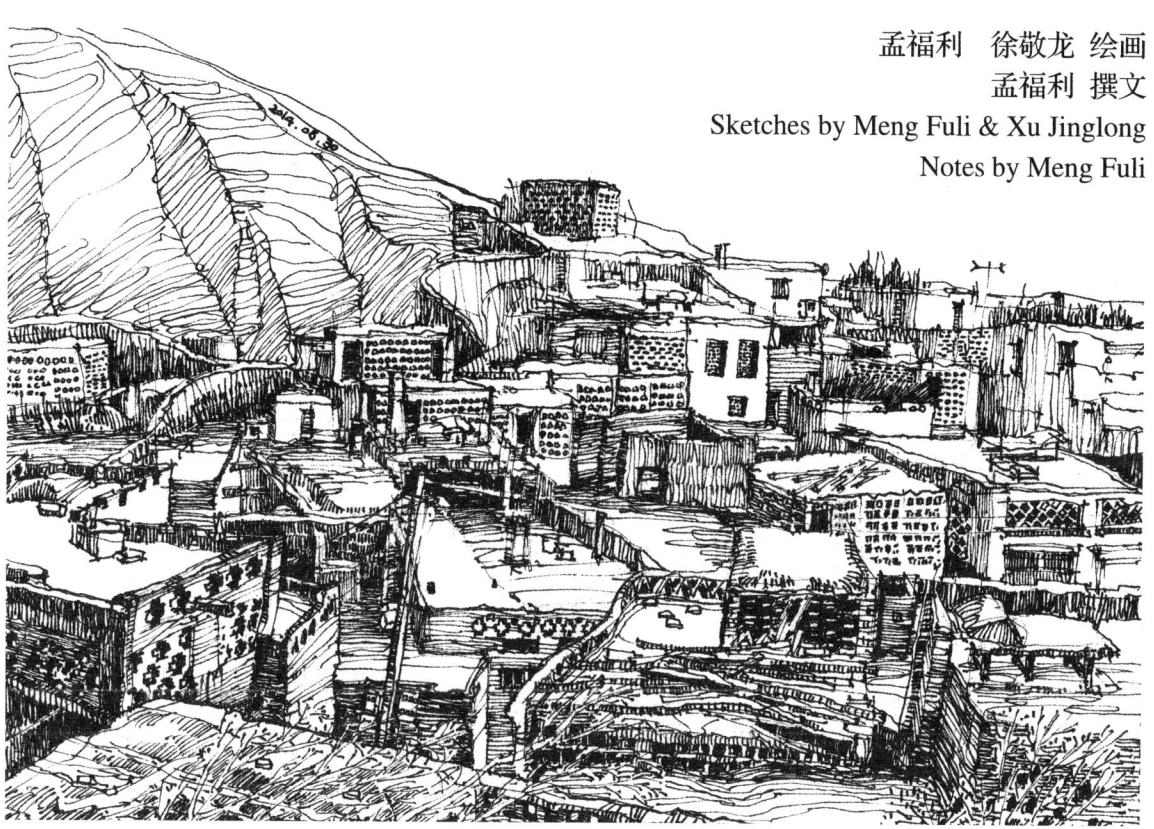

学苑出版社
Academy Press

图书在版编目（CIP）数据

天山南部风情 / 孟福利, 徐敬龙绘画、撰文. — 北京：学苑出版社，2017.5
（故园画忆系列）
ISBN 978-7-5077-5235-9

Ⅰ.①天… Ⅱ.①孟…②徐… Ⅲ.①风俗习惯—介绍—新疆
Ⅳ.①K892.445

中国版本图书馆CIP数据核字（2017）第136649号

责任编辑：	周　鼎
编　　辑：	陈柯宇
出版发行：	学苑出版社
社　　址：	北京市丰台区南方庄2号院1号楼
邮政编码：	100079
网　　址：	www.book001.com
电子信箱：	xueyuan@public.bta.net.cn
联系电话：	010-67601101（营销部）、67603091（总编室）
经　　销：	全国新华书店
印　刷　厂：	北京信彩瑞禾印刷厂
开本尺寸：	889×1194　1/24
印　　张：	5
字　　数：	120千字
图　　幅：	99幅
版　　次：	2017年7月北京第1版
印　　次：	2017年7月北京第1次印刷
定　　价：	45.00元

目　录

自　序　　　　　　　　　　　　　　孟福利

历史·建筑

交河故城	3
柏孜克里克石窟	4
高昌故城方形佛塔	5
二塘沟唐代烽燧	6
营盘古城遗迹	7
小河墓地	8
苏巴什佛寺遗址	9–10
克孜尔尕哈烽燧	11
民丰尼雅遗址	12
艾提尕尔清真寺	13
艾提尕尔清真寺内部	14
喀什的土城门	15
阿帕克霍加麻扎旁边的小清真寺	16
莫尔佛塔	17
艾提卡尔大清真寺	18
吐峪沟清真寺	19
清真寺	20
清真寺的宣礼塔	21
朝圣之路	22
天宫伎乐残陶片	23
无首残缺佛像	24
图木舒克佛像头部	25

乡土·建筑

麻扎阿里蒂村·鸟瞰	29–32
麻扎阿里蒂村·街巷	33–40
麻扎阿里蒂村·爬山屋群	41
麻扎阿里蒂村·露台	42–45
麻扎阿里蒂村·葡萄晾房	46–48
麻扎阿里蒂村·葡萄晾房内部	49
麻扎阿里蒂村·过街楼	50–53
麻扎阿里蒂村·高侧窗	54–55
麻扎阿里蒂村·古桑树	56–57
麻扎阿里蒂村·墓地	58–59
高台民居	60–68
巴里坤民居·村落	69–73
巴里坤民居·院落	74–78
和田民居·干栏式	79–84
和田民居·阿以旺式	85–86

民风·民俗

小憩的老人	89
驼队和牵驼人	90-91
驴车和牵驴人	92-93
都塔尔艺人	94
玉石匠人	95-96
土陶艺人	97
编筐人	98
卖葫芦的人	99
打馕人	100
卖馕人	101
弹花人	102
织毡氇的人	103
纺织作坊	104
织机	105
剃头匠人	106

Contents

Forward   Meng Fuli

Historic Architecture

Jiaohe Ancient Town	3
Bezeklik Caves	4
Square Pagoda in Gaochang Ancient Town	5
Beacons of Ertanggou in the Tang Dynasty	6
Yingpan Ancient Town Site	7
Homeland of the Deceased	8
Subashi Temple Relics	9-10
Keziergaha Beacons	11
Minfeng Niya Site	12
Id Kah Mosque	13
Id Kah Mosque Inside	14
Soil Gate of Kashgar	15
Small Mosque next to Apak Huojia's Tomb	16
Moore Stupa	17
Aitikal Grand Mosque	18
Tuyugou Mosque	19
Mosque	20
Mosque Minarets	21
The Pilgrim	22
Incomplete Pottery Statue	23
Headless Buddha Statue	24
Head of Buddha Statues in Tumushuke Temple	25

Vernacular Architecture

Map of Mazha Village · Bird's Eye View	29-32
Mazha Village · Street Space	33-40
Mazha Village · House Groups up to the Mountain	41
Mazha Village · Terrace	42-45
Mazha Village · Grapes Hanging Room	46-48
Mazha Village · Indoor View of Grapes Hanging Room	49
Mazha Village · Arcade	50-53
Mazha Village · High Side Window	54-55
Mazha Village · The Ancient Mulberry	56-57
Mazha Village · Cemetery	58-59
Dwelling Houses on Cliffs	60-68
Balikun Residence · Hamlet	69-73
The Barkol Areas Residence · Courtyard	74-78
Hotan · Bannister Style Houses	79-84
Hotan · Ayiwang Style	85-86

Folk Customs

The Resters in Mosque	89

Camel Team	90-91	Nang Maker	100
Donkey Cart	92-93	Nang Seller	101
Dutar Player	94	Cotton-fluffing Worker	102
Jade Craftsman	95-96	Pulu Woven Carpet People	103
Pottery Craftsman	97	Weaving Workshop	104
Basket Knitter	98	Loom	105
Gourd Seller	99	Barber	106

自　序

新疆地域辽阔、地形地貌类型多元化，多民族聚居，具有古老文明多样并存与整体灿烂的特点。随着城镇化进程的加快，新疆具有代表性的文化景观，如东疆吐鲁番地区的生土民居、反映人类杰出智慧的水利工程——坎儿井，南疆和田地区的阿以旺民居、喀什地区的高台民居、古代军事设施遗存等，面临着即将消逝的境地。因此，针对东疆和南疆传统聚落进行保护与发展研究的必要性日益凸显。

本书试图从新疆东疆和南疆地区选取具有代表性的历史文化村镇，从村镇建筑、民俗技艺、古代建筑遗存等层面，记述东疆和南疆的风情。作为新疆民居研究的工作者，我希望本书能够对新疆传统建筑、文化景观遗产保护工作具有一定的积极意义，同时通过生动的图像语言，让更多人对新疆的地理特征、民居艺术、民俗风情等有更多的认知。本书是国家社科基金艺术学资助项目"城镇化进程中的新疆绿洲型历史文化村镇景观风貌保护与发展研究"项目（14CG126）的阶段性成果之一，同时也是石河子大学新疆非物质研究中心的文化遗产研究工作的部分成果。适合传统民居爱好者；建筑学、环境艺术设计学相关学科作为民居艺术、民俗遗产等研究的参考教材使用。

本书的出版，离不开领导、同事及朋友们的帮助与协作。我要感谢学苑出版社给我提供这次机会，使得我们有动力来完成这项工作。特别要感谢洪文雄编辑，从选题策划、内容甄选等方面给予的帮助；感谢周鼎编辑为本书提供的指导性建议；感谢我的老同学同时也是本书的作者之一的徐敬龙，他不仅对场景选取和图绘工作提出了关键性的意见，且书中主要作品也由他亲自完成。最后，要感谢我的学生们为本书提供图片整理及图稿描绘等帮助。

　　本人学识水平有限，书中难免存在许多不足之处，敬请读者斧正。

孟福利
于石河子大学
2016年3月28日

Forward

Xinjiang is a vast, multi-ethnic populated region with diversified topography and geomorphic attributes. Various ancient civilizations coexist here with overall brilliantness. With the acceleration of the urbanization process the representative cultural landscapes in Xinjiang (such as the raw soil dwellings in the Turpan area of Eastern Xinjiang, the water conservancy project Karez which reflected the outstanding wisdom of human being, the Ayiwang dwelling in the Hetian area of Southern Xinjiang, the terraced dwelling in the Kashgar area and the famous ancient military facilities) will no longer exist soon. Therefore, the necessity of researching on protection and development of the traditional settlements in eastern and southern Xinjiang is increasing.

This book attempts to select representative historical and cultural towns and villages in eastern and southern Xinjiang to record the dwelling styles through drawings and words focused on three aspects of rural architecture, ancient folk art and architectural remains. As the residential researcher of Xinjiang, I hope this book will have certain positive meaning on heritage protection work of traditional architecture and the cultural landscape in Xinjiang while helping more people to know more about geographical characteristics, art of folk houses and folk customs of Xinjiang. This book is one of the primary achievements of project Research on the Protection and Development of Landscape Features of Oasis Historical and Cultural Towns and Villages in the Process of Urbanization in Xinjiang (14CG126) financed by National Social Science Fund. It is also partial results of cultural heritage research of Xinjiang Intangible Culture Center of Shihezi University. It is suitable for being used as reference materials on studying the art of dwellings and folk customs heritage by traditional dwelling enthusiasts, architecture and environment art design students.

This book could not be published without the help and cooperation of my leaders, colleagues and friends. I would like to thank Academy Press for giving me this opportunity and especially thank Editor Hong Wenxiong, who offered great help with the planning, topic selection, and content selection. I would also like to thank Zhou Ding for guidance and suggestions on the content and publishing related issues. Further, I want to thank Mr. Xu Jinglong, who was my former classmate and is the coauthor of this book. He gave crucial comments on scene selection, drawings and drew most of the drawings in this book. Last but not least, thanks to my students who sorted out the drawings. Without the help from the above aforementioned people, this book could not be completed on time. Due to my limited knowledge, there must be deficiencies in this book. Any comments or corrections would be appreciated.

Meng Fuli
From Shihezi University
March 28, 2016

历史·建筑
Historic Architecture

交河故城

位于吐鲁番市雅尔乡将格勒买斯村，是世界上最大、最古老的生土建筑城市遗址，也是我国保存2000多年最完整的都市遗迹。唐西域最高军政机构安西都护府最早就设在交河故城。

Jiaohe Ancient Town

Located in Jianggelemaisi Village, Yaer Town, Turpan City, it is the largest and oldest town built by rawsoil in the world as well as the best preserved city ruin with a history of over 2000 years in China. Anxi Frontier Command, which was the supreme military and political institution in the western region during the Tang Dynasty(618-907) was set up in Jiaohe Ancient Town.

[柏孜克里克石窟]

位于吐鲁番市东45千米的火焰山脚下。始凿于南北朝后期，经历了唐、五代、宋、元长达7个世纪的漫长岁月。石窟以内嵌式佛龛阵列排列，形制规格较高。这里一直是高昌地区的佛教中心，目前是新疆境内较大的佛教石窟寺遗址之一。

Bezeklik Caves

Located at the foot of the Mountain of Flames, 45 kilometers to the east of Turpan City, Xinjiang, it was firstly excavated during the late Northern and Southern Dynasties(420-589) and existed for 7 centries. The embedded niches were arrayed inside the cave with higher shape specification. It had been the Buddhist center in the Gaochang region. It is currently one of the larger Buddhist cave sites in Xinjiang.

交河故城方形佛塔

位于吐鲁番市西郊10千米处的雅尔乃孜沟村。该塔位于高昌故城遗址的城市主轴线上。塔基为方形，中心是主塔，四周由小塔拱卫，整体形态壮观浑厚。

Square Pagoda in Jiaohe Ancient Town

Located in Yaernaizi Village, 10 kilometers to the west of Turpan City, the pagoda was on the main shaft line of the city and has a square base. The main pagoda is in the center and is surrounded by smaller pagodas. The whole appearance is grand and lively.

二塘沟唐代烽燧

位于鄯善县连木沁镇,在巴哥庄西北约5500米处。因位于天山南麓二塘沟口的冲积扇面上,又名巴哥塔。该烽燧为土坯建筑,平面呈方形,剖面呈梯形。

Beacons of Ertanggou in the Tang Dynasty

It is located on the alluvial fan of Ertangou, southern foot of Tianshan Mountain, 5.5 kilometers to the northwest of Bage Town, Shanshan County. It is also known as Bage Tower. The beacon is built by adobe with square in plan and trapezpid in section.

营盘古城遗迹

　　位于巴音郭楞蒙古自治州东南部，兴地山以南的戈壁滩上。这里是公元138年西域三十六国之一的山国的都城，丝绸之路北道的必经之地。整个古城呈圆形，直径350多米，占地面积约9.5万平方米，被历史学家称为"第二楼兰"。

Yingpan Ancient Town Site

Located in the Gobi Desert, Southern Xingdi Mountain, Southeastern Bayinguoleng Mongolian Autonomous Prefecture, Yingpan Ancient Town was the capital of Shan Kingdom, one of the 36 kingdoms in the Western Regions in 138 and the necessary way to Northern Silk Road. The ancient town is a circle with 350-meter-diameter and occupies an area of 95,000 square meters. It is called Second Loulan by historians.

小河墓地

位于罗布泊地区孔雀河下游河谷南约60千米的罗布沙漠中，东距楼兰古城遗址175千米，距今已有3500多年历史。墓地整休由数层上下叠压的墓葬及其他遗存构成，是平缓的沙漠中突兀而起的一个椭圆形沙山。小河墓地被世界考古学界认为是中亚历史上沙埋文明之谜。

Homeland of the Deceased

Located in the Luobu desert, 60 kilometers downstream in t he valley of Peacock River, 175 kilometers to western Loulan Ancient Town, with a history of over 3500 years, the cemetery consists of layers of tombs and other remains. It is an oval-shaped sand hill abruptly erected in the gentle desert and is regarded as the mystery of civilization buried in sand in the history of middle asia by international archaeological circles.

苏巴什佛寺遗址（一）

　　位于阿克苏地区库车县城北20千米处。始建于4世纪，又称昭怙厘大寺、雀离大寺。分东、西二寺，分布于铜厂河东西两岸冲积台地上，主体建筑群已消逝在戈壁中，只剩下少量遗存。东寺依山而筑，寺垣已毁。寺内有房舍和佛塔遗迹，全系土坯建造，房舍墙壁高者达10余米，寺内有三座高塔。西寺中依断岩处有一小围墙，呈方形，周约318米，亦土坯筑，残高10米以上。图一为西寺佛塔遗存，图二为东寺佛塔遗存。

Subashi Temple Relics (1)

Twenty kilometers to Northern Kuche, Aksu, the temple consists of East and West temples and was originally built in 4th Century with names as Zhaoguli Temple and Queli Temple. It is located on the alluvial platform of the Kuer River and only small part remains while main buildings have vanished into the Gobi Desert. The East temple was built along the hill and the columns are destroyed. There are 3 tall pagodaes, houses and pagoda relics made by adobe in the temple. The walls of the houses are as high as over 10 meters. In the West temple, there is a small square bounding wall made by adobe with perimeter of 318 meters and remaining height is over 10 meters. Picture 1 shows the remains of pagoda in West temple and picture 2 shows the remains of pagoda in East temple.

苏巴什佛寺遗址（二）

Subashi Temple Relics (2)

克孜尔尕哈烽燧

位于库车县依西哈拉乡境内，东南距库车县城10千米。建于汉代，烽燧基底平面呈长方形，东西长6米，南北宽4米。是目前古丝绸之路北道上时代最早、保存最完好的烽燧遗址。

Keziergaha Beacons
Located in Yixihala Town, Kuche County, 10 kilometers to Kuche downtown, it was built in the Han Dynasty (25-220) with a rectangular base that is 6 meters long and 4 meters wide. It is the oldest and best preserved beacon relics on northern Silk Road.

民丰尼雅遗址

位于塔克拉玛干沙漠南缘民丰县喀巴阿斯卡村以北20千米的沙漠中，是公元前2世纪至5世纪精绝国故址。目前遗址除发现90多处房屋以外，还发现有佛塔、古桥、墓地、果树园、寺院、手工作坊、家畜饲养舍、田地、林阴路、河床等遗迹，而且还保留着大量的枯树林。

Minfeng Niya Site

Located in the desert 20 kilometers to the north of Kabaaska Village, Minfeng County, Southern Taklimakan Desert, the Minfeng Niya site was from the Jingjue kingdom in the second century B.C. to the 5th century B.C.. Besides more than 90 houses, many relics were also found in the site, such as a pagoda, an ancient bridge, a cemetery, fruit garden, temple, manual workshop, livestock shed, fields, an avenue and a riverbed. A lot of withered trees are well preserved as well.

【艾提尕尔清真寺】

位于喀什市的艾提尕尔广场西侧，始建于1442年。南北长140米，东西宽120米，占地总面积为1.68万平方米，分为正殿、外殿、教经堂、院落、拱拜孜、宣礼塔、大门等七部分。它是新疆规模最大的清真寺，在全国的清真寺中，其规模也位居前列。

Id Kah Mosque

Located in western Id Kah Square of Kashgar, it was built in 1442 with a length of 140 meters, a width of 120 meters and a total area of 16,800 square meters. It is divided into seven parts. They are the main hall, outside hall, lectern teaching hall, courtyards, an arch, minarets and a gate. It is the largest mosque in Xinjiang and one of the nation's largest mosques.

艾提尕尔清真寺内部

艾提尕尔清真寺的顶部为穹顶。穹顶四周为高侧采光、通风窗，造型为拱券式，内嵌于厚实的生土墙内，内景整体颇为壮观。

Id Kah Mosque Inside

The top of the mosque is dome. There are arched, high windows all around. The windows are embedded in the thick wall of raw soil and the overall interior view is quite spectacular.

喀什的土城门

位于喀什市老城区东侧。经过数代经营,至1906年形成此规模,是当时出入喀什古城极为重要的关口。现无存。

Soil Gate of Kashgar

Located in the eastern old town of Kashgar city, it was an important pass for going in and out of Kashgar in old times but doesn't exist today.

阿帕克霍加麻扎旁边的小清真寺

  位于喀什市东北郊5000米处，是伊斯兰教"霍加"（即圣人后裔）安葬地的附属建筑之一。寺前有彩绘天棚覆顶的高台，高台后面有祈祷室，供附近信徒日常做礼拜之用。

Small Mosque next to Apak Huojia's Tomb

Located at 5 kilometers to northeastern Kashgar City, it is one of the attached buildings of Huojia's burial place. Huojia means descendants of Saints. There is a tall tower covered by a colorful painted ceiling in front of the mosque and a prayer room behind for believers to pray daily.

莫尔佛塔

位于喀什市东北约30千米处。始建于唐代，距今已有1000多年的历史。该塔由一座椭圆形土塔和一座覆斗形高台构成。土塔中空，高12米多，下有三层方座，以土坯砌筑而成。土塔旁边的巨大高台，是这里的中心建筑，专门用来供佛。

Moore Stupa

Located 30 kilometers to northeastern Kashgar City, it was built in the Tang Dynasty (618-907). The stupa consists of an oval shape soil tower and a covered bucket-shaped terrace. The soil tower is hollow and 12 meters high with 3-layered square foundation made by adobe. The giant terrace next to the tower is the center of the building and it is dedicated to worshiping Buddha.

艾提卡尔大清真寺

位于于田县境内，距今有800多年的历史。屋顶有两个观望塔和一个圆形顶棚，做工精巧。是和田地区规模较大的一座穆斯林宗教活动场所。

Aitikal Grand Mosque

Located in Yutian County, it has a history of over 800 years. There are two watch towers and one round roof on top of the building in delicate craftmanship. It is a large venue for Muslim activity in the Hetian region.

吐峪沟清真寺

　　这幅小景是在去吐鲁番吐峪沟乡的途中完成的。起初是被肌理丰富而色彩赭红的火焰山所吸引,当转过身后,发现了远处高岗的清真寺,于是用笔记录下这一场景。它孤立于高岗之上,像远航中的灯塔指引着方向。

Tuyugou Mosque

This drawing was completed on the way to Tuyugou Town, I was first attracted by the rich texture and color of the Mountain of Flames and only found the mosque erected on the high mountain after I had turned back. It stands on the mountain alone and looks like a lighthouse guiding boats towards the right direction.

清真寺

　　清真寺在维吾尔族传统聚落中是必不可少的公共空间形式之一，具有邻里之间感情交流、信息传播、信仰的表达与寄托等功能。清真寺的选址通常是地势平坦、交通便利的地方，民居则分布在清真寺的周围，久而久之形成"围寺而居"的布局形态。

Mosque

The mosque is one of the essential forms of public space in the Uyghur traditional settlements with the functions of emotional exchange, information spread, expression and sustenance of believes between neighbours. The location is usually on flat ground nearconvenient transportation. Dwellings are distributed around the mosque and form the layout of "living around the mosque".

清真寺的宣礼塔

位于吐鲁番吐峪沟乡。塔身挺拔，砖饰以菱形图案为主，色彩自然古朴，典型的伊斯兰教公共建筑形式。

Mosque Minarets

Located in Tuyugou Town, it is a tall and straight tower with a diamond pattern on the bricks. It is typical of Islamic public architecture With natural and primitive colors.

> 朝圣之路

　　顺着这段山路，可以到达"七圣徒"的墓地，看似不起眼的一段路，却有着深刻的意义。

The Pilgrim

This mountain road leads to the Seven Saints Cemetery. The ordinary-looking road, however, has a profound significance.

【天宫伎乐残陶片】

出土于和田地区约特干遗址,现存英国伦敦大不列颠博物馆。

Incomplete Pottery Statue

Unearthed from Yuetegan site in the Hetian region, the pottery statue is collected by the British museum in London.

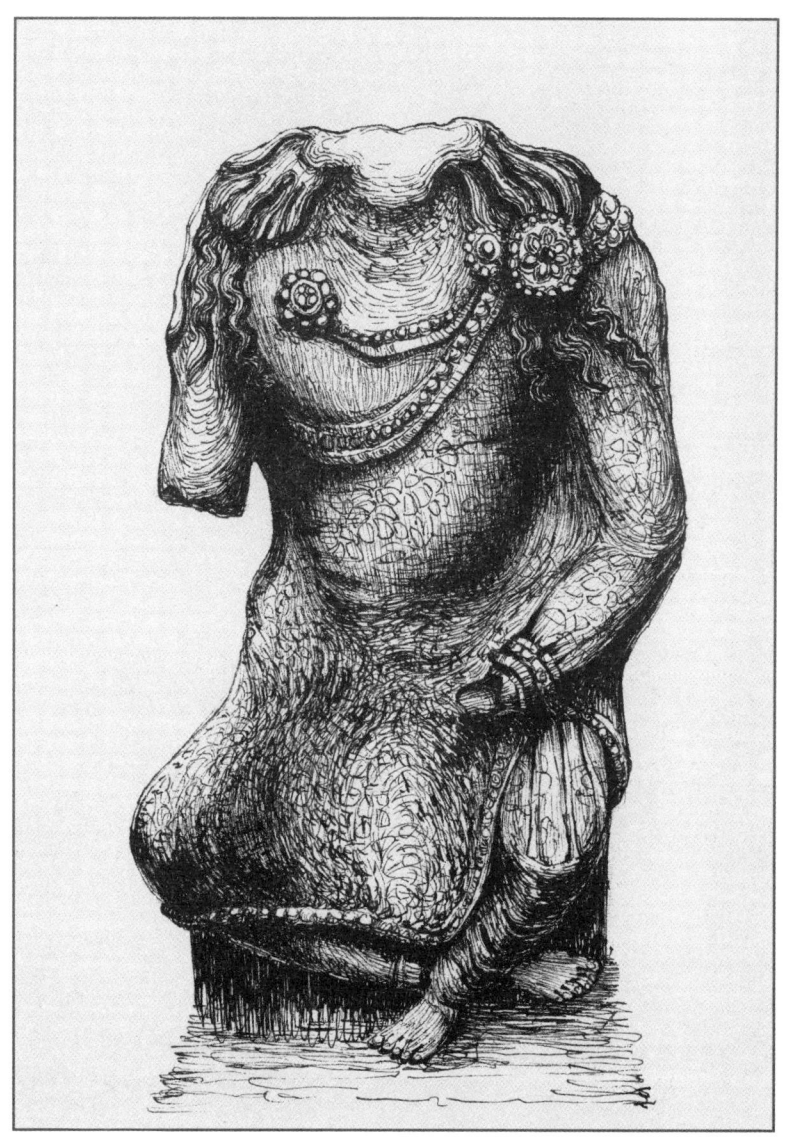

无首残缺佛像

这是一尊南疆地区出土的无首残缺佛像。此佛像体型壮硕，线条流畅而优美，盘膝而坐，身着轻盈的贯首长裙，肩部以石榴花、玫瑰花配流苏装饰，造型富丽而规整的饰带具有中亚艺术风格。

Headless Buddha Statue

This is an incomplete statue of Buddha without a head unearthed from southern Xinjiang. This figure of Buddha is heavy and has smooth and elegant lines. The Buddha sits with crossed legs and a light, long dress. There are pomegranate flowers decorating his shoulder and roses with tassels on his chest. The richly exquisite and neat beaded lace is in the central Asian art style.

图木舒克佛像头部

这尊4世纪末期的佛陀出土于图木舒克市图木舒克佛寺遗址，1906年被法国探险队所获。佛首头顶为磨光式肉髻，面容丰满慈祥，从佛像的造型特征来看，吸收了古印度佛像艺术特征，同时又具有西域本土佛教艺术特点。

Head of Buddha Statues in Tumushuke Temple

Head of Buddha Statues in Tumushuke Temple This statue of the Buddha was unearthed from Tumushuke temple in Bachu county of Southern Xinjiang and gained by a French expedition in 1906. It was scarved in late 4thcentury.The Buddha has a broad forehead and peaceful expression with a polished topknot on the head. All these showed that it was influenced by ancient Indian Buddha art while boasting the characteristics of the western local Buddhist art.

乡土·建筑
Vernacular Architecture

麻扎阿里蒂村·鸟瞰（一）

位于吐鲁番东部鄯善县吐峪沟乡，简称麻扎村，是吐鲁番地区最古老的维族村落。该村落背依火焰山，一条小河从北向南穿村而过。麻扎村的先民根据当地的自然环境和生存需要，就地取材，充分、巧妙地利用黄黏土造房，渐渐形成了以生土为主要材料的建筑特点，该村落集生土建筑之大成，是国内保存完好的生土建筑群之一。

Map of Mazha Village · Bird's Eye View (1)

Located in Tuyugou Town, Shanshan County, the east of Turpan, with a short name as Mazha, it is the oldest Uygur village in Turpan region.The village was built in frontof the Mountain of Flames with a creek flowing through from north to south. Based on the local natural environment, the ancestors of Mazha village built houses with the local material-yellow clay and it gradually became the architecture features of Mazha village. Mazha village is an agglomeration of raw soil buildings and is one of the well-preserved raw soil building groups in China.

麻扎阿里蒂村·鸟瞰（二）

Map of Mazha Village · Bird's Eye View (2)

麻扎阿里蒂村·鸟瞰(三)

Map of Mazha Village · Bird's Eye View (3)

麻扎阿里蒂村·鸟瞰(四)

Map of Mazha Village · Bird's Eye View (4)

麻扎阿里蒂村·街巷（一）

　　麻扎村建筑依据地形而建，边界有的凸出，有的凹进，凸出和凹进的错位就形成小的阴凉空间。随着时间推移，逐渐形成了适宜干热区气候特点的"凸凹"街巷空间。生土作为天然的建筑材料，压土成坯、夯筑成墙、掘土成室等加工都是遵循了材料本身的物理属性，营造的生土街巷体量浑厚，如堡寨一般。

Mazha Village · Street Space (1)

The buildings in Mazha Village were built based on the natural terrain, with convex-concave borders. The dislocation of protruding and concave sections formed small, cool spaces-and with time goes by, they gradually formed convex-concave street space suitable for the dry and hot climate. The local people used raw soil as a kind of natural building material and followed its physical properties to compact it into bricks to build walls while digging rooms and building raw soil streets as thick as their village walls.

麻扎阿里蒂村·街巷（二）

Mazha Village · Street Space (2)

麻扎阿里蒂村·街巷（三）

Mazha Village · Street Space (3)

麻扎阿里蒂村·街巷(四)

Mazha Village · Street Space (4)

麻扎阿里蒂村·街巷（五）

Mazha Village · Street Space (5)

麻扎阿里蒂村·街巷（六）

Mazha Village · Street Space (6)

麻扎阿里蒂村·街巷（七）

Mazha Village · Street Space (7)

麻扎阿里蒂村·街巷（八）

Mazha Village · Street Space (8)

麻扎阿里蒂村·爬山屋群

该村位于火焰山山谷的冲积扇上。随着人口的增多，民居建筑逐渐在山坡高处营建，久而久之，就形成了如今阶梯错落的爬山屋的建筑类型，成为地域特色建筑景观类型。

Mazha Village · House Groups up to the Mountain

The raw soil settlement of Mazha Village is located on the alluvial fan plain in the valley of the Mountain of Flames. With the increase of the population, local-style dwellings started to be built on the hillside, gradually. It formed the building groups arrayed on the hillside like random ladders and it has become characteristic of the regional architecture.

麻扎阿里蒂村·露台（一）

  吐鲁番地区的生土村落建筑通常为平屋顶，适应干热少雨的气候。在平屋顶上，人们开辟出了露台这一多功能附属空间形式。在屋顶周边设置简易的木栅格做安全围护，顶部架设高棚架，形成围合的室外空间。夏季，白天可以在此做简单生产，晚上可以纳凉休息。

Mazha'alidi Village · Terrace (1)

Raw soil settlements in the Turpan region are usually built with flat roofs to adapt to the dry and hot climate. Flat roofs are also used as terraces by local people. In the summer, they can do some simple production on the terrace while enjoying the cool air and, later in the evening, they can rest there.

麻扎阿里蒂村·露台（二）

Mazha'alidi Village · Terrace (2)

麻扎阿里蒂村·露台（三）

Mazha'alidi Village · Terrace (3)

麻扎阿里蒂村·露台（四）

Mazha'alidi Village · Terrace (4)

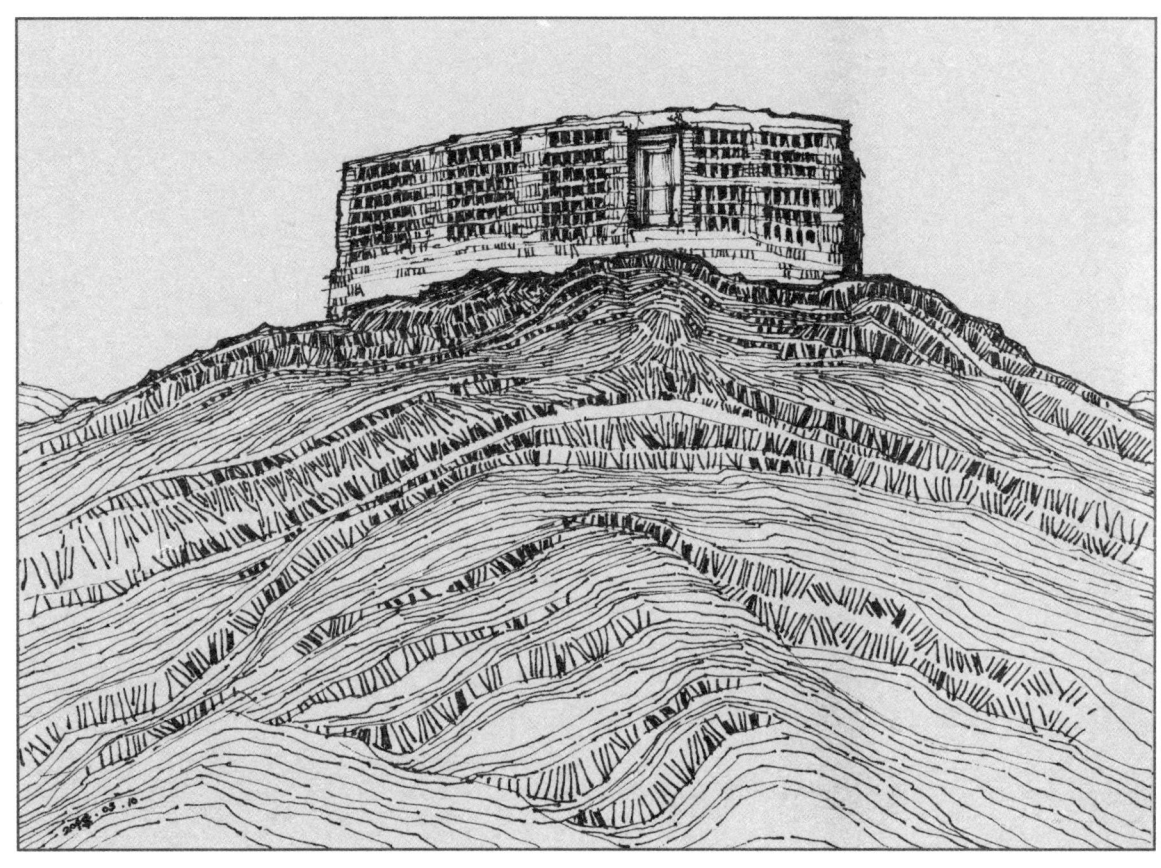

麻扎阿里蒂村·葡萄晾房（一）

葡萄晾房是吐鲁番地区独具特色的生产性建筑，它是先民利用土坯砖砌筑成的利于通风的花墙式建筑。葡萄晾房通常建在二楼，也有建在高岗处的，甚至有建在过街楼上的，以充分利用空气的对流作用。此图为建在高山上的葡萄晾房。

Mazha'alidi Village · Grapes Hanging Room (1)

As a unique productive building in Turpan, the grape hanging room is a kind of flora wall built with adobe bricks and with good ventilation. They are usually built on the second floor, mound or even on archade to make full use of air convection. The drawing shows the grape hanging room built on the high mountain.

麻扎阿里蒂村·葡萄晾房（二）

Mazha'alidi Village · Grapes Hanging Room (2)

麻扎阿里蒂村·葡萄晾房（三）

Mazha'alidi Village · Grapes Hanging Room (3)

麻扎阿里蒂村·葡萄晾房内部

葡萄晾房内部通常用枣树枝作为晾架。在枣树枝上面悬挂葡萄，利用自然风来阴干葡萄，做成葡萄干。

Mazha'alidi Village · Indoor View of Grapes Hanging Room

Inside the grape hanging room, Chinese jujube branches are usually used as drying racks and grapes are hung on all branches. It uses natural hot air convection to dry the grapes in the shade and the grapes turn to easily-preserved raisins.

麻扎阿里蒂村·过街楼（一）

在建筑材料匮乏的年代，人们利用土拱式建造技术来解决房屋的跨度问题。在修二楼时，将楼延伸出去跨过小街小巷搭建到对面的建筑上。这种颇具创造性的建筑形式逐渐被推广开来，经过数百年，渐渐形成了特有的"过街楼"景观。

Mazha'alidi Village · Arcade (1)

Local people solved the problem of limited space by building raw soilarcades in a time when building materials were scarce. When building the second floor, they stretched the floor out across the lanes. Such an innovative architectural form was gradually popularized and formed a unique arcade landscape after hundreds of years.

麻扎阿里蒂村·过街楼（二）

Mazha'alidi Village · Arcade (2)

麻扎阿里蒂村·过街楼（三）

Mazha'alidi Village · Arcade (3)

麻扎阿里蒂村·过街楼（四）

Mazha'alidi Village · Arcade (4)

麻扎阿里蒂村·高侧窗（一）

　　从高处望过去，麻扎阿里蒂村的房屋土墙上排列着大大小小的高侧窗，这是麻扎阿里蒂村建筑构件的一大特色。厚实的生土墙可以隔热保温，高侧窗则益于防风沙，交换空气。这一建筑形式是当地人与自然互动的结果，反映了人们利用自然资源应对气候条件的智慧。

Mazha'alidi Village · High Side Window (1)

Looking down from above, there are high side windows in different sizes on the walls of houses and it is the architecture feature of Mazha'alidi village. The thick, raw soil walls work as heat insulators and high, double-layer windows are used to avoid sand and high winds from blowing in while exchanging the air. This architecture style is the result of the interaction between local people and nature. This reflects the wisdom of people using natural resources to fight against climate condition..

麻扎阿里蒂村·高侧窗（二）

Mazha'alidi Village · High Side Window (2)

麻扎阿里蒂村·古桑树(一)

吐鲁番地区为西域古代高昌国所在地,典籍记载此地为西域诸国中植桑养蚕最早的地区。树龄百年以上的桑树,在吐鲁番传统乡村聚落中比较常见,是当地乡土景观特色之一。它们大多出现在聚落主要公共空间的节点处,起到聚合公共空间,满足人们休憩、交流等作用。

Mazha'alidi Village · The Ancient Mulberry (1)

Turpan is the site of ancient Gaochang Kingdom in Western Region and according to ancient record, it was the region of the earliest mulberry bush plantings and raising of silkworm .The over-100-year-old mulberry bushes are common in traditional villages in Turpan and it is one of the features of local landscape. The bushes were usually planted in the joint of main public spaces and made the public space ideal for people to have a rest and communicate with each other, etc.

麻扎阿里蒂村·古桑树（二）

Mazha'alidi Village · The Ancient Mulberry (2)

麻扎阿里蒂村·墓地（一）

"麻扎"是阿拉伯文语音译，意为"圣地""圣徒墓"，主要指伊斯兰教显贵的陵墓。麻扎的造型有别于生者的建筑，易于识别。规格较高的，通常为方基座，上为穹顶，以生土拱券而成。

Mazha'alidi Village · Cemetery (1)

Mazha means Holly Land or Tombs of Holly Muslim in Arabic. It mainly referres to the tombs of Islamic dignitaries. The shape of Mazha is different from the building for the living and easy to identify. The tombs usually built by raw soil with square base and arch top.

麻扎阿里蒂村·墓地（二）

Mazha'alidi Village · Cemetery (2)

高台民居（一）

高台民居是一种传统的维吾尔族建筑形式。房屋依崖而建，家族人口增多一代，便在祖辈的房上加盖一层，这样一代一代，房连房、楼连楼，层层叠叠。喀什老城现存许多百年以上土木混合结构的高台民居建筑，通常为两层，在一层顶部加挑台，形成与室外过渡的连廊空间。

Dwelling Houses on Cliffs (1)

Dwelling house on cliff is a kind of traditional uygur architecture with houses built on the cliffs. With an increasing family population, local residents built additional floor on top of the old house and the house connected to each other with tiers upon tiers. There are many over-100-year dwelling houses on cliffs with civil mixed structure in old town of Kashgar. They are usually 2-storey houses with balcony on top of the first floor forming the transitional space to the outdoors.

高台民居（二）

Dwelling Houses on Cliffs (2)

高台民居（三）

Dwelling Houses on Cliffs (3)

高台民居（四）

Dwelling Houses on Cliffs (4)

高台民居（五）

Dwelling Houses on Cliffs (5)

高台民居（六）

Dwelling Houses on Cliffs (6)

高台民居（七）

Dwelling Houses on Cliffs (7)

高台民居（八）

Dwelling Houses on Cliffs (8)

高台民居（九）

Dwelling Houses on Cliffs (9)

巴里坤民居·村落（一）

巴里坤草原位于新疆东北部的哈密地区，是新疆的第二大草原。这里水草丰美，地势平坦，为优质的山间草甸牧场。该区域的建筑，以原木材建造为主，形式融合了中原营造风格，屋面呈"人"字式，院落围墙以原木堆叠而成，构造结实，经济耐用。

Balikun Residence · Hamlet (1)

Located in Hami region, northeastern Xinjiang, Balikun grassland is the second largest grassland in Xinjiang. The rich, fresh green grass and flat ground make Balikun grassland a premium mountain pasture. The houses in this area are mainly made by logs with the style of the central plains. The roof is in the shape of the Chinese character for "people" and the compound walls are piled by logs. It is a solid construction but also economic and durable.

巴里坤民居·村落（二）

Balikun Residence · Hamlet (2)

巴里坤民居·村落（三）

Balikun Residence · Hamlet (3)

巴里坤民居·村落（四）

Balikun Residence · Hamlet (4)

巴里坤民居·村落（五）

Balikun Residence · Hamlet (5)

巴里坤民居·院落（一）

　　巴里坤大草原自汉代以来就是进入古代西域的军事与屯田重地，受中原居住文化的影响，这里的游牧定居点的院落形式与中原相似，与吐鲁番地区的院落建造形式有重大差异。其典型特征是坡面屋、围合的院落，吸收了中原地区封闭、紧凑的建筑特征。

The Barkol Areas Residence · Courtyard (1)

The Balikun grassland has been an important military fortified point leading to the western region since the Han Dynasty(25-220). Affected by the residential culture of the central plains, the courtyards of nomadic settlements here are similar to the central plains, but have significant differences from the settlements in the Turpan area. The building's sloped roof and closed yard is characteristics of the regional style and they originated from the closed and compacted form of central plains.

巴里坤民居·院落（二）

The Barkol Areas Residence · Courtyard (2)

巴里坤民居·院落（三）

The Barkol Areas Residence · Courtyard (3)

巴里坤民居·院落（四）

The Barkol Areas Residence · Courtyard (4)

巴里坤民居·院落（五）

The Barkol Areas Residence · Courtyard (5)

和田民居·干栏式（一）

和田地区的民居主要有干栏式、阿以旺式两种。泥抹笆子墙建造工艺是干栏式民居的主要特征之一。当地人以木材为骨架，辅以生土、秸秆等填充主要建筑墙体。

Hotan · Bannister Style Houses (1)

Bannister style and Ayiwang style are two main styles of dwelling houses in Hotan region. Walls supplemented by raw soil and straw is the main characteristic of bannister style houses. Local residences use wood as skeleton of the house and walls are supplemented by raw soil and straw.

和田民居・干栏式（二）

Hotan · Bannister Style Houses (2)

和田民居·干栏式（三）

Hotan · Bannister Style Houses (3)

和田民居·干栏式（四）

Hotan · Bannister Style Houses (4)

和田民居·干栏式（五）

Hotan · Bannister Style Houses (5)

和田民居·干程式（六）

Hotan · Bannister Style Houses (6)

和田民居·阿以旺式（一）

阿以旺式是一种带有天窗的房屋样式。这种房屋连成一片，庭院在四周。带天窗的前室称阿以旺，又称夏室，有起居、会客等多种用途。后室称冬室，是卧室，通常不开窗。住宅的平面布局灵活，室内设多处壁龛，墙面大量使用石膏雕饰。

Hotan · Ayiwang Style (1)

Ayiwang is a kind of house with skylight. These houses are linked to each other with a courtyard around them. The front chamber with skylight is also called summer room which can be used as living room and reception room. The back room which is called winter room is bedroom with windows closed usually. Residencial layout is flexible with several niches indoor and vast gymsum scarving on the wall.

和田民居·阿以旺式（二）

Hotan · Ayiwang Style (2)

民风·民俗
Folk Customs

小憩的老人

　　清真寺，亦称礼拜寺，是穆斯林举行礼拜、宗教功课的中心场所和交往中心。穆斯林间有关婚姻、遗产、商业等纠纷，通常也都在清真寺内按教法规定解决或调处。唐宋时期称清真寺为堂、礼堂，元代以后称礼拜寺，明代称清真寺，沿用至今。图为和田某清真寺内一景，做完礼拜的老者正在小憩。

The Resters in Mosque

Mosque is the main place for Muslims' worship and religious events as well as communication center. Disputes related to marriage, inheritance and business are usually solved or conciliated according to Islamic law in the mosque. The mosque was called Hall in the Tang (618-907) & Song(960-1279) Dynasties while being called Worship Temple in the Yuan Dynasty(1206-1368). Since the Ming Dynasty(1368-1644), it has been called Mosque. The drawing shows the seniors taking a rest after worship in a mosque in Hetian.

驼队和牵驼人（一）

骆驼被人们比喻为"沙漠之舟"，在古代中西方经济、文化交流的悠悠古道上，发挥了极其重要的作用。而带领骆驼商队走过沙漠的牵驼人，比常人有着更多的毅力和坚强。图为喀什老城东侧门广场一景，等待出发的牵驼人，背景是生土夯筑的城门。

Camel Team (1)

The camel is compared to transportation in dessert and played extremely important role in economical and cultural exchanges between China and Western countries in ancient time. Camel-leaders, who lead camel caravan walking through desert, usually are more determined and stronger than ordinary people. The picture shows camel-leaders are ready to depart in front of the town gates made by raw soil in eastern sauare of old town in Kashgar.

驼队和牵驼人（二）

Camel Team (2)

驴车和牵驴人（一）

新疆的驴耐粗饲、耐酷暑、耐严寒；驴车曾是新疆旧时重要的交通工具。维吾尔族老汉唱着歌、赶着驴车，带着家人去赶巴扎（集市），曾是新疆一景。目前在偏远的地区，驴车仍然是重要的交通工具。该图是喀什一景，驴车上拉着皮料。20世纪80年代，从事皮具制作的匠人还很多。

Donkey Cart (1)

Donkeys in Xinjiang are resistant to roughhuge, intense heat and bitter cold. The donkey carts were important means of transportation in old days. It once was a scene in Xinjing that an uygur old man was riding a donkey cart to bazzr with his family while singing. The donkey carts are still important means of transportation in remote areas today. The drawing shows a leather worker is leading a donkey cart with leather materials in Kashgar. In 1980's, there were many leather workers in Kashgar.

驴车和牵驴人（二）

Donkey Cart (2)

都塔尔艺人

都塔尔是维吾尔族钟情的民间弹弦乐器,其名字来源于波斯语,意为两根弦的乐器。传统的都塔尔多用桑木、杏木或核桃木制作,规格尺寸分为男、女和儿童用三种。都塔尔音色柔美,弹奏出来的声音比较小。图为喀什市街边的都塔尔艺人在弹唱。

Dutar Player

Dutar is the favorite folk instrument of uygur people. Its name originally from Farsi which means instrument with two strings. Traditional dutar was made by mulberry, apricop or walnut wood with different sizes for men, women and children. The sound of dutar is gentle and beautirul. The picture shows an artist is singing while playing the Dutar in the street of Kashgar.

玉石匠人（一）

"昆仑产美玉，匠人遍市井。"从事玉石加工的手艺人，在南疆地区较为常见，技艺世代相传。图为玉石作坊里的匠人在加工玉石。

Jade Craftsman (1)

Kunlun mountain is famous for fine jade stones and Jade craftsmen with skills inherited from generation to generation arecommon in Southern Xinjiang. The picture shows craftsmen are cutting jade stones.

玉石匠人（二）

Jade Craftsman (2)

土陶艺人

在喀什地区从事土陶营生的人很多。极其普通的黄土，在土陶艺人的手里会变成一件件盛水的器皿，或是装点空间的精致的工艺品。

Pottery Craftsman

There are many people engaged in the earthenware business in the Kashgar region. The extremely common loess can become water vessels or exquisite art and crafts through the hands of the pottery craftsman.

　　南疆绿洲上盛产红柳、梭梭等枝条柔韧的多年灌木，为生产生活提供了丰富的原料。图为街边的编筐者。

Basket Knitter

In the oasis of Southern Xinjiang, bushes with flexible branches are flourishing. They provide rich raw materials for production and life. The picture shows a basket knitter along the street.

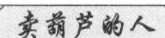

卖葫芦的人

在干热的南疆地区，葫芦是盛放水的容器，也是彼此馈赠的礼物。图为和田某巴扎（集市）上卖葫芦的老者，悠闲地等待着客人。

Gourd Seller

In hot and dry Southern Xinjiang, the gourd is a container for water, as well as a gift. An old gourd seller is leisurely waiting for customers in the bazaar in Hetian County.

打馕人

馕在新疆食品中历史悠久,古代称为胡饼、炉饼。2000多年前自西域传入中原,东汉时甚至在宫廷里都曾兴起过胡饼热。馕具有便于携带、久存不坏的特点,是古代西域商旅行人的最佳选择。馕大部分在馕坑里烤成,形状多为圆形,芯薄边稍厚。烤馕的技术在维吾尔族人中几乎是普及的,无论男女都会做馕。

Nang Maker

Nang is a kind of food with long history in Xinjiang. Known as Persian pancake or stove pancake, Nang was introduced to central plain from western region 2000 years ago. In East Han Dynasty(25-220), it was very popular in royal court. Nang was the best food for business travellers in ancient western region as it was easy to carry and could be stored for a long time. Most Nang are baked in Nang pit in round shapes with thinner middle part and thicker edge. The skill of baking nang is very common in uygur people and almost everybody can bake it.

[卖馕人]

　　新疆城市、乡间，到处都有馕坑和馕饼店，馕饼摞得高高的，馕香四溢。维吾尔族对馕有很多禁忌，比如不允许数个数；掉在地上的馕渣要拾起来放在高台上给鸟儿吃；结婚时新郎和新娘要吃醮着盐水的馕，象征有福同享、白头偕老。在维吾尔族人眼中，馕就是生命。他们有句名言："馕是信仰，无馕遭殃。"

Nang Seller
There are Nang pits and Nang shops everywhere in Xinjiang, no matter in cities or countrisides. The Nangs are piled highly with good smell spread around. Uygur people have many taboos on Nang, such as to count the Nang is not allowed, the crumbs on the ground should be picked up and put on the high platform to feed birds, The groom and bride should eat the Nang with salty water in the wedding which represents to share the blessing and grow old together. In the eyes of Uygur people, Nang is the life. They have a saying as "Nang is the belief and life without Nang is suffering. "

弹花人

　　弹棉花是一种老手艺，随着一声声弦响、一片片花飞，最后把一堆棉花压成一条整整齐齐的被褥，仿佛就是一种魔术。新疆的棉花为优质长绒棉，制作出的产品质地柔软。目前，在南疆的很多地方，弹棉花的手艺人依然大受欢迎。图为和田的一位弹花人正在劳作。

Cotton-fluffing Worker

Cotton-fluffing is a kind of traditional skill. With the sounding string and flying cotton, a pile of cotton becomes neat quilts finally. It is like a kind of magic. The cotton produced in Xinjiang is quality long-staple cotton and good for making soft quality bedding. Cotton-fluffing workers are still popular in Southern Xinjiang. The drawing shows a cotton-fluffing worker is working in Hetian County.

织毯氆的人

氆氇是一种古老的毛织物,结实耐用,保暖性好,在高寒地区多用。过去,织氆氇用的是老式木棱织机。织好的氆氇一般是白色的,用大黄、荞麦和核桃皮等染成赭红、黄、绿等颜色。图为昆仑山山前戈壁地带的普鲁村的妇女正在织氆氇。

Pulu Woven Carpet People

Pulu is a kind of traditional wool fabric popular in cold areas for its durability and warmth. In the past, Pupu was woved by traditional wooden loom in white color and dyed byRhubarb, buckwheat and walnut skin. The drawing shows women of Pulu Village, located in Gobi desert in front of Kunlun mountain, are weaving Pulu.

> 纺织作坊

　　在南疆的传统营生中,纺织行业曾经最为辉煌。《喀什乡土志》记载:"沿街十铺。二三桑营也。"现今已很少有手工织造布匹,机器加工的织物成了主流。

Weaving Workshop

The textile indus try once was the most brilliant industry among traditional industries in Southern Xinjiang. According to local record of Kas hgar, "two or three among ten shops along the street are silk shops." Nowadays, weaving cloth by hand is rare and, machine-made fabric has became the mainstream.

织机

种桑纺丝、撵毛成线、种花搓绒这些解决东疆、南疆世居者的穿衣戴帽的手作活动，在传统聚落中最为常见。长长的丝线像一根根文化的脐带，连接着古丝绸之路的过去与未来。

Loom

Mulberry planting, silk spinning, cotton planting and textile productiion were the most common activities in the traditional settlement and supplied clothes for residents in eastern and southern Xinjiang. Long silk thread is like the cultural umbilical cord connecting the past and future of the ancient Silk Road.

剃头匠人

南疆各地的巴扎（集市）上都能看到剃头匠的身影。图为一位维吾尔族剃头匠在帮客人修面。

Barber

In southern Xinjiang, barbers can be seen in every bazaar(market). The sketch shows an old Uygur barber who is shaving for a guest.